THE KINGDOM WHERE NO ONE DIES

©2025 Jeff McRae

All rights reserved. Printed in the United States of America. Except as permitted under the United States Copyright Act of 1976, no part of this publication may be reproduced or distributed in any form or by any means, or stored in a database or retrieval system, without the prior written permission of the publisher.

ISBN 979-8-9902208-9-8

Cover by Tom Eykemans
Cover art by Francis Colburn (1909-1984); Charley Smith and His Barn, ca. 1939; Collection of the Bennington Museum, Bennington, Vermont

Book design by Nord Compo

Published by Pulley Press

Pulley Press is a nonprofit that promotes and celebrates rural poets and poetry.

Learn more at www.pulleypress.com

THE KINGDOM WHERE NO ONE DIES

JEFF McRAE

*Thanks to Derek Webster, Fran Lunney,
and Amy Schroeder for their expertise, encouragement,
and enthusiasm over the many years of writing
and editing these poems.*

*Special thanks to Andrew Johnson for his decades
of friendship.*

*To my mom, dad, and sister—I hope I've told
our story well.*

*Finn, Charlie, and Wren—I am so fortunate
to be your dad.*

For Erin

Contents

Dedications xi
Epigraphs v
Acknowledgments 1

PART 1

Crowned 5
Sitting on a Hay Bale 6
Filaments 7
Night Pasture 9
The Doctor is Out 10
The Kingdom Where No One Dies 12
Dark Chocolate 13
Motion Detector 14
Cognitive Dissonance 16
College Try 18
Astronaut 20
I Found a New Baby, Lake George, 2019 21
New Year's Day 23
Coming up Jesus 24
Kurt Vonnegut Stepped off the Plane 26
Wedding Band 28
Stan Getz, Stockholm, 1988 29
Musicians in Breughel's *The Peasant Wedding* 30

PART 2

A Kind of Promise 35
Rooted 37
Echo Location 38
Origami 41
Cults 42
Deadhead Riot 44
Skunked 45
Skin 46
Bolt Stunner 47
Dream Box 48
Dennis Gonyaw 50
Cheap Guitar 51
At the Cemetery 52
The Song Inside 53
First on the Scene 55
Highly Regarded 56
Taking Our Son to College in the Morning 58
Jeopardy 59
Cymbal 60
Symbols 61
Animal Hospital 62
University 64
Fair Game 65

PART 3

The Heart's Bones 69
Meagre Objects 71
To Things Left Behind 73
In Situ 74

History of Square Dancing 76
Winter Fuel 77
The Summer My Sister Channeled the Spirit World 79
Span 81
Father's Desk 82
La Vie en Rose 84
Against Feeling 86
The Lesson 87
Asleep 89
Scrimshaw 90
Picking Stone 92

About the Author 94

Once left alone,
You and I, dear, will go with softer steps
Up and down stairs and through the rooms...

—**ROBERT FROST**, "In the Home Stretch"

The one who lights the wood stove
Gets up in the dark.

—**CHARLES SIMIC**, "February"

Acknowledgments

Some poems appeared or are forthcoming in the following journals, sometimes in different forms:

A-Minor Magazine	... "Crowned"
The American Journal of Poetry	... "Dennis Gonyaw"
	... "Fixing the Motion-Detector Light"
	... "The Lesson"
Antioch Review	... "Animal Hospital"
Ascent	... "The Song Inside"
Beloit Poetry Journal	... "Picking Stone"
Briar Cliff Review	... "In Situ"
Burnside Review	... "Echo Location"
Cider Press Review	... "At the Cemetery"
The Chariton Review	... "Against Feeling"
	... "The Doctor is Out"
	... "Scrimshaw"
Cloudbank	... "Dream Box"
	... "Sitting on a Hay Bale"
The Common	... "La Vie en Rose"
Euphony Journal	... "Coming up Jesus"
Hayden's Ferry Review	... "The Kingdom Where No One Dies"
I-70 Review	... "Father's Desk"
	... "Dark Chocolate"

The Lilliput Review	... "Skin"
Main Street Rag	... "Deadhead Riot"
Massachusetts Review	... "History of Square Dancing"
The Maynard	... "Astronaut"
The Midwest Quarterly	... "Winter Fuel"
The Mind's Eye	... "Symbols"
	... "To Things Left Behind"
	... "Wedding Band"
Mudfish	... "Skunked"
	... "Night Pasture"
North Dakota Quarterly	... "Highly Regarded"
	... "Taking Our Son to College in the Morning"
	... "University"
Northern New England Review	... "Filaments"
	... "Rooted"
One Art	... "Span"
Permafrost Magazine	... "New Year's Day"
Poetry South	... "The Summer My Sister Channeled the Spirit World"
The Raleigh Review	... "A Kind of Promise"
Rattle	... "Cheap Guitar"
	... "Cognitive Dissonance"
	... "Jeopardy"
	... "Kurt Vonnegut Stepped off the Plane"
Salamander	... "Musicians in Breughel's 'The Peasant Wedding'"
	... "College Try"
Sheila-Na-Gig Online	... "Origami"
Woven Tale Press	... "The Heart's Bones"

Part 1

Crowned

There was music but we meant
magic. Magic of the tall grass
and the open door, in our spells

when we crossed the earth, noses
in the smoke. We whistled,
puckered up and stunned the birds

with words we called urges.
They lifted us. They filled us
when we were face forward for

the fifty things. Even falling down
they sounded like a crown
of sonnets, how we got up over

and over, majestically, looking
over the edge of the bed saying
I love love love you. Later

evening grew like a bruise.
Then night swooped in how you
pull a lover aside and share

the secret you've held so long
it's become unreal, an ancient
bell, a peal, a song, a sing along.

Sitting on a Hay Bale

You wanted me to get a job but I wanted to play my washboard. You were a respected mid-career professional with a reputation and 401k and I had my washboard and brief moments on the bandstand when all eyes fell on my thimbles rattling out the flams, ratamacues, and polyrhythms. That's what we were, you and I—a pair of pulses that felt like they would never align but always did given time. You wanted to watch David Beckham on Netflix and I shouted through the window, *Give me a minute to finish my concerto with these glorious backyard birds!* You wanted happy children as did I. I said so with my washboard hanging round my neck like a medal of honor, light as a lei. Between those syncopated sentences I hugged it to my chest. I loved my washboard. It was Adam and I the Assembler of Parts—bell, cymbal, and body like the edge of a sculpture Michelangelo couldn't resolve, a figure unreleased from stone until I played and all the barn doors of the past opened and I seemed to sit on a musty bale with fiddlers and snakes speaking in tongues.

Filaments

Mother sends an email: The Farm is Up For Sale Again.
Inside, a blue link to the listing I don't want to click.

I click. I'd heard the house was gone but never made
the pilgrim's trip to see the empty space formerly

filled with our stairwell, bookshelf, piano; the mirror
in which we primped and posed for dates after chores,

where we waged wars with solitude and work. The faint
odor of manure on my coat, kitchen floor slippery

with chaff. It's all more than a memory can house—
where we argued, listened, read aloud after dinner,

heard, saw, slept and woke up. Out back, the old
walnut held me with one arm above the hedge like

a gentle god holds a boy who lives in a world
of animals and long grass—all of it bulldozed out

of our lives except the spring house, its constant
cascade into a wellspring that feeds all living things

on the now *former dairy with two barns and
scenic views.* Thank god the grandparents are dead

and not alive to see this vulgar snowbird nest,
potential Airbnb investment property. Trees grow

in the field for Christ sake. Their cabin, built up
the road redone, done up, gentrified. Who knew

how strong the limb that held me there. One point
seven million for it all. The final filaments

of ownership are imaginary. And true, it's been
too long to see we were there—not in the meadow

edge, fields we cleared, tree line we cut. Not
in the cement we poured, the "Welcome Home"

painted on the barn bay door when Father was gone
for weekend gigs. I've mourned, held it proudly.

I'm worn thin with the whole thing. What do I betray
by putting it down, the memory—that farm, our

childhoods, the story of who I've been convinced
we were? I'm never going back. I shut my eyes

and walk the road into the dooryard. There is
the old house, front door askew in its jamb.

The dining table set with Mother's plates and
we're all there, the dog on my foot, my glass

full of raw milk.

Night Pasture

Thirty years since Father
sold up and moved us
off the farm. The falling
apart is long over but we
remain expert in the things
we no longer own: mountain
and river; the road named
after us and our forebears
who cut the timber,
pulled stone from the field;
who drained the swales,
dug the run-off; who raised
barns and bought the herd;
fed it and children; cleaned
trout in the springhouse;
tried pigs, chickens, a horse,
kept a bull; who rotated
cattle from hidden piece
to night pasture. Two long-
handled shovels, a hoe,
and a pitchfork—
I keep them, propped
in a corner of our garage.

The Doctor is Out

Weren't those just the days
of overcooked food,
constant lack of toilet paper?
Every moment was crucial:
someone slapped your face,
you lost the rhythm,
you fell down in the street.
A boy in blue overalls
traced your outline
with his yellow chunk of chalk.
An enormous flock of starlings
appeared from a tree.
You were an outline suggesting a body.
Your shoes were on the wrong feet.
You were torn in all directions.
Should you confess or say nothing?
Bite your tongue, cry out?
Your mouth was full of sores.
You loved women
who loved other men.
You photographed a calf.
Someone watched you from a window
while you listened to rock,
drank shit red wine
and threw it up late at night
alone in the woods.
You found a ten dollar bill and lost it.
You wailed and didn't want

company. You smoked
brand cigarettes then rolled your own
then went back to brand.
You tried hard to form an idea
stopped at a red light
car humming beneath you.

The Kingdom Where No One Dies

Because we were to move away
and never come back,
I decided to climb the big tree
in the front yard.

A man strolled the sidewalk.
I'm moving today, I told him.
The neighbors crept out of their houses.
A bird perched on my shoulder.
I laughed, but by now
the sky had grown dark.
No one came to look for me.

The bird built a nest
in my hair. By morning
I could hear it, full of hunger.
The bird grew up and flew away.

A little girl climbed up beside me.
I'm your daughter, she said.
She gave me the smallest
penknife in the world.
It's up to you, she said.

Dark Chocolate

Important people owned houses
filled with games and wine.
Jesus lived on the biggest cloud—
a tall dark one full of rain.
That was our idea that time

we stared across the valley,
the untouchable clouds thin,
blood-red streaks. We were good
at the store, quiet in the car
with hunks of dark chocolate

melting in our mouths.
Jesus visited important people
all over the sky. We had
no idea why. Who cleaned
his robes? Proteins were hard

to wash. He sat criss-cross
applesauce on the cloud
smiling over all children.
I see you—buckle up! Mother
and Father let us think like that.

Motion Detector

I stamp my boots harder than usual
to announce my arrival inside his home.

The old tone of knowingness.
What's one more mechanical failure.

Climb in the truck and roll
down the rain-ruined drive

to test the wires. Heft the new axe,
dirty the new shirt, snap the new pen.

Everything wears out, everything grows
beyond repair.

He suspects the fault lies with him.
No need to spend money on that.

No more surgeries, no more stents.
No more spare-part solutions.

Laddie, I want the big one to come,
he says, twisting his hands

like he's breaking a chicken neck.
His own neck.

We stand together,
rain drumming on the tin roof,

addressing our mutual problem.
Everything gets broken.

After cribbage, he says, *Come back soon.*
The yellow light blinks across the yard.

Cognitive Dissonance

Jesus Christ, I just hit that fucking bird, I said
though the car was empty. It was that beautiful,
whatever it was: long, mottled white and brown,
fanned-out, straining to make it. A bird's brain

is small, its head made the tiniest thunk on the fender
and then it disappeared: no cloud of feathers,
no tumbling wings on the road, no claw in the grill.
For a second, just before it died, it was spectacular.

That's how death should be. I was telling someone
a NASA engineer brought a black tile in a bag
to Mr. Morelli's seventh grade science class.
Just like the ones used on the Challenger, he told us

and blasted it with a torch, and the blue flame splayed
across it like the wing of a jay. Then he pointed
the flame away, our fingers stunned
by the tile's hard cold. We put it together: the tile

resisted the heat like nothing had happened,
as though he never struck the match
igniting the gas and the jet of flame never
touched the tile. Something had happened—

we saw it but we could not believe.
Morelli sat back like a cat that ate a bird.
A week later, I was drinking milk in the hall
with Scott and Jason when he hustled by:

The shuttle just blew up. That was progress and industry
and good government and science and education
all at once. We knew it was a lesson
about aspiration and how it can end up

on the bottom of the sea. Morelli rolled the TV
on its gurney to the front of class and we watched
the split-screen news: sky scribbled with smoke/
students watching Christa McAuliffe vanish.

College Try

I was disconcerted when she asked me
to throw her against the wall of her
studio apartment since we just met
in the hall of her complex. *Do it.*
I won't mind, she said, barely touching
my arm. We sat on her homework.
I was like a dandelion that popped up
overnight. What if she put a hole
in the sheetrock with her head?
Experimenting college kids—mescaline,
ménage à trois, skinny dipping with eels?
None of it was part of my repertoire.
Girls back home did not ask me
to throw them around. I could
unhook a bra, kiss a neck, sing S+G
on solo guitar. We were all old friends,
since kindergarten. This girl was more
Mrs. Robinson in her loose-fit jeans
and pinstriped vest. She didn't want me
to push her against the wall of that
low-lit room fouled by patchouli
and Lisa Loeb and stare darkly
into her eyes à la Darcy. *Do it.*
I'd built a respect for my high school
sisters—we ranked each other's butts,
made out in the dugout, explored
bodies in a logged-off wood lot.
Small town farm boys and girls

we drove nails, hay wagons,
or a fast ball deep, deep, deep
and gone. By the time we left home
everybody knew every body. Sure,
you were going to cry a little bit
but nobody got seriously hurt.

Astronaut

Shhh. I'm about to wake up.
My legs are floating
out of bed—where is

yesterday? Who sold me
this trash? I will
not finish hammering
this shoddy life together.

All I really am doing:
drinking Tang
four days a week.

The most
important poem
I can write you says,
Pick up the kids.

I must be standing
in the attic
counting down to blast off.

A strange life they lead,
astronauts: mashed
potatoes and gravy
every meal.

I Found a New Baby, Lake George, 2019

Cognoscente call it contribution,
call it *conversation*. But some cats don't
listen, don't want to hear what you say.
For some it's all one way. Like Bill
who speaks in tongues. *Satan lives
in a hole so deep it can't be plumbed.*
I haul my drums to the grass. We know
about the earth—lakes of fire deep inside,
don't we? He looks knowing and locks
the truck door. He won't play any
"modern stuff." No ambiguity. His solos
say the same thing no matter what
the form or style: *Let God in and you
live forever! A pretty good deal.*
We wrap with an up-tempo stomp
through "I Found A New Baby."
Later, he pays with a hundred dollar
bill. *See? Bill bestows.* We load up
then cross the Hudson into the tangle
of upstate. One hour in he says,
*I can hold out five dollars and say,
"Take these five dollars." But you must
reach out and take the five dollars.*
Bill says I am more Christian than
a lot of people in the dark. Thanks
very much, I reply noting night is
a dark time for us all and that that
was a hell of a ride meaning I can't

believe in ghosts. Undaunted, he helps
me lug my drums. Thanks for driving,
I say, ten bucks for gas inside my
handshake. *I'm going home,* he says,
and pray you take that five dollars.
Then I'm going to sleep like a baby.

New Year's Day

The last time
we got wasted
he said I looked
prayerful. I am,
I lied. In college
he preached no
elbows on the
table, chased
his Ritalin with
orange juice. Now
he's dead but not
before I envied
his millions. Two
hundred some
odd people died
in the city the
day he leapt/fell
into Starbucks
from eleven
windows up.
Who knows how
religious he felt.
One woman
said she would
never forget his
blood on her shirt.

Coming up Jesus

Jesus had it going on for a good couple of years,
like Billy Collins—followers who said mmm when
he hit them with a perfect image, event attendees
who snapped their fingers and played bongos,

who caught him up when he took the leap of faith,
held him over head, passing him person to person
like something viral, a Best of the Net poem. Never
did they let him fall. And just like Collins they

wanted to touch him, be near when he left the stage
for dinner and drinks at the after-hours hang with
like-minded locals. Jesus toured a solid year, playing
small venues (hilltop, outside town, tonight!),

growing his base, hustling, honing his cadence,
tightening his timing, before hitting it big, always
performing the same material but changed it up
gig to gig, tweaks to make it new, keep his own

interest, working out other angles on love. At first,
reviews were few but his reputation grew and by
what accounts remain he killed, he slayed—
seekers arrived early and stayed late. Oh sure,

some nights they threw stones or soldiers cleared
the olive grove. Even Billy wrote a stinker or two.
For Jesus, parables were the glue for the whole
show—without them he was just another weirdo

standing in a river with a ragtag entourage. But there was no doubt—the man was on to something, all au courant—all these feelings you didn't know you already knew and had never told a soul.

Kurt Vonnegut Stepped off the Plane

Sipped from his flask crossing the shoals and my girlfriend
drove him to campus. She was always involved with

something and I was involved with her, showed up
at the studio Sunday morning when she painted her post-

modern trees, followed her to the African textiles show.
Stop trying to make yourself cry, she said when she

dumped me. Vonnegut followed her around for the afternoon.
She bought him ice cream with a couple dollars from

the student group petty cash. They speculated about the age
of the oak on the quad all while he accepted small mouthfuls

of praise. I broke out in hives. No poems—not mine
nor those of Wordsworth—were going to bring her back.

It was fucking over. Done. I didn't have a chance
to play her the version of "Moon River" I'd worked up

for our hump day movie night. Vonnegut took the stage
in a stupor and rambled in and out of amplification,

from poetry to the art of fame. It was about becoming
he explained at the end of his talk, trussing his dangling ideas,

taking everyone's breath. *Become a better person.*
Years passed. She wrote me an old fashioned letter.

I wrote back. We had three children. This morning
she told me the dog threw up on the rug last night.

I descended the stairs thinking even what you fling
far away, like some primitive weapon, returns.

Wedding Band

The bride and groom throw open the door
so we *uh-one two three fah!*
kick the Steppenwolf
and the Harleys fire their guns
and the drive wheels spin
and a noxious plume of exhaust
and rubber fills the yard.

She slips into the circle
of heavy metal thunder, teeth glinting
like a crash cymbal, a quartet of daisies
in hand, looking for adventure
beneath a black leather sky.

He enters a different life—
hands held, senses bursting:

and the tube amps crunch and pop
and the biker drops to a last longer gear,
engine roaring like a dive-bomber
and the tire explodes and the party screams

and fists pump and rebels yell
and beer spits into the sky
and we're smoking the oldies
like it's the first time
and the charred logs roll off the bonfires,
going up in smoke as
fast as nature allows.

Stan Getz, Stockholm, 1988

You might think
we are like

whales—song
flowing over

beds of salt-
water grasses

then into deep
water, heard

by other whales
turning into

the lachrymose
miles seeking

its source—
but we are not.

Musicians in Breughel's *The Peasant Wedding*

One, shadow-faced, gazes at the food, mouthpiece
fallen from his slice-of-life lips. Three silver charms

dangle à la beads of sweat from his hat. It's hot as a barn
in the hall. Any musician knows what that's like.

A musician sees that and recalls all the jobs with guys
who can't read, smoke hash with the groom, or drink

between sets and advance on the bride. A wedding
is rote, a living for these two depicted the moment

dessert arrives—the hunger on his face tells you that,
lacks pretense. A musician needs only a brief glimpse

to recall sleeping in his car outside the Y, building
a reputation at the guild for arriving early

with a pencil. They met at a festival or feast day
or one heard the other from the street and paused—

who is that? where has he been hiding? Thus bands
are born. Wheat sheaves cross on the wall. Feathers

hang from the bagpipes, instrument for peasants
without crumhorn or shawm. The common musician

earns union scale. This young player rests his weight
on one foot in classical pose, obviously knows

celebration is business. It's not his first wedding.
The dagger strapped to his back tells any musician that.

Part 2

A Kind of Promise

Rain falls on the gymnasium roof
and we sit five minutes with the
lights off, listening. Hunger seeps
into the second grade. Thunder
rumbles in the unseen sky. Her daddy
packed a box of raisins for lunch.
I really like your short hair!
I can see eggs. They've lived there
since last year, her nape bloody
with bites. Across the ceiling
and down the walls, pipes channel
the water around our make-due rows.
I slip a set of watercolors I bought
the night before into her desk and say,
*Paint me a picture of your favorite
animal.* Two days later she brings
a dream, a unicorn. Her family
was kicked out of Tennessee.
The whole thing, she says. It's a
mythic place she remembers as
the sound of cars outside a motel.
The global pandemic landed us
in the gym where last year a string
section played Mendelssohn and
years ago my son hit the winning shot
on a dead ball foul. Now we're rows
and columns beneath the cranked-back
backboard, the net netting a papier-

mâché butterfly like some changed
and beautiful fragile thing. Every
metamorphosis is a promise.
We're learning to make change,
to read, to write haiku, to predict
how many almonds fit inside a jar.

Rooted

I call Mother on Sunday afternoon.
Hellooooo, how are you?! I ask,
afraid she is lonely on her new floors,
with her HVAC set for summer
sixty-five. It looks like rain,
make sure to bring your laundry in,
she says. I am two hundred
miles away and there are no clouds
in the sky above my house, mom.
Just an airplane. Why not go?
I say, resuming our argument
that she visit the ocean. What
are you waiting for? I stay in
my lane and do not welcome
change but, all the same, I root
for her to go to Maine, to York,
Portland, or points further north,
place names we know from
a children's book she read
to me when we were young.
I hear thunder over the phone.
It's starting to rain, she says. It's so
beautiful sliding down the window.

Echo Location

In my mind, I'm forking
hot lunch into the mouth
of seven-year-old Fritz Hughbacher
not well-behaved and faced
with many problems he recounts
at the end of the schoolyard
over a dead owl. Poor Fritz—

bags under his eyes
and the wrong team jacket.
How do I tell you about his eyes?
A nebula of capillaries coursed
with plum-colored blood like
he'd been punched in the face.
Illness was crossing off his days

and I was overwhelmed
by long division (divide three
weeks of winter vacation by
seven days, divide each day
by twenty-four hours, each hour
by sixty minutes, and minutes by
how many seconds until we see

each other?). I learned to cross
my sevens like they did in Oslo,
a great grey city crossed by flocks
of grey migrating geese. During

the cold recesses of second grade
we copied definitions of interesting
illustrations: *Old Faithful, fissure,*

fjord—where mountains
of migrating ice slowly slashed
through rock and sheets of snow
frosted a pitchy stave church.
Humans hiked three days
through wolves to pray in that
windowless dark, said the dictionary.

Fritz said sun warmed the *fjordland.*
Fritz said during day the sun
was a shiner and in evening
the sun was a bloody eye.
Fritz, I can barely see you
through all this accumulated
time, behind your coke bottle

lenses, eyes large and luminous
as an owl's. Fritz, your nose is runny.
Fritz, you hang from the bus door
the Friday before Christmas,
telling me something I can't hear
over the engines, your quiet cloud
memory's empty caption.

Then you climb the two tall steps,
the yellow door unfolds shut
like a map opening across a desk,

and the bus pulls away forever.
Can you see how far I've traveled
today? From Shelburne to Oslo
I am the only person on earth
thinking of you.

Origami

In fourth grade the students discover
the forest around their house. They hear
many birds singing together. Even the dead tree
contains living birds. In fifth grade
they sit in a row on the jungle gym,
protecting their nests. They speak to each other
like babies to mask a silence—they fear
the ugly bird inside. Soon everyone's nest is full
of broken eggs. No one speaks about them.
In fifth grade the student learns to fold paper,
to establish with the precision of a crease
where one edge envelopes another edge.
They fold crane after crane. They do it
every morning until they create a flock
of one thousand quiet birds. They wish
to never leave. The classroom is a school.
The classroom is a storm. They look at the waves.
They look at the thunder. Everyone knows
which birds are theirs. They fill their backpacks
and bring the birds home. Cranes line the windowsill,
fill the glass bowl. Mobiles turn in the draft.
It takes all of sixth grade to fold a fox.
They gift it to their parents. In seventh grade
the forest is silent. The child is gone.

Cults

In the cool English building basement I listed "C.J."
as the classmate with whom I wanted most
to write the research essay with. We pushed
our chairs into a group of two and uncovered
a shared interest in cults. The campus priest told us
local groups infiltrate the student body *often*.
Signs your roommate was being drawn into a cult:
they ceased taking calls from family or letters from home
lay unopened on the desk. We'd know they were in danger
if they suddenly gave their clothes away *or if they stop
drinking beer with you* the priest said with a wink.
If they cut their driver's license up, adopt the name
"Crow," and pedal around like Jesus Christ on a bike,
they were probably ok. I would have given up a lot
if I could get with C.J. and perform rituals.
Some cult behavior seemed within bounds—
didn't I know what it was to maintain a desire
in the dark of the body? *We have the best project
in the whole class*, she whispered one night
close to my ear outside the library and, I believed her.
We cultivated an interest in a lecture—"Jesus, Mary
Magdalene, and the Wine of Samara." Pen in hand
we wandered like outsiders through the vanilla
undergrads but I couldn't deny other students were
catching my eye, smiling at us. *Go talk to them*,
she prompted, squeezing my arm. I did, with a strange
sense of being desired. After we recorded our impressions
in moonlight. *The group displays unquestioned*

commitment to the leader, she read aloud. I nodded,
breathless. We wrote up our findings and I offered
my pen, my phone, use of my laptop; I could get rid
of my roommate if she needed a quiet place to think—
I'd get take-out, find us some beer.

Deadhead Riot

The street was jammed with fruit
flies, deadheads selling shrooms,
and poorly made glassware. I thought
my folks had split up. I thought sex
in a tent was the be all. I thought
the Dead were a waste of money.
I thought D.H. Lawrence was
hilarious on Whitman. I thought
I knew my way around. And then
I spotted Father and his brother
walking up the street like a pair
of little boys in tie-dye shirts
trailing two gigantic blue balloons
of nitrous. We were waiting to rush
the gates. Why did we drive
all the way to Highgate with no tix?
They thought that was funny as hell.
The Penis Bus drove by full of
topless hippy girls dropping flowers
and buds on the heads of all
the frat boys who would never
have a chance of stepping foot
on board. My girlfriend said that
was stupid and walked off. My dad
held his balloon between his teeth
and I was torn in all directions. The
gate was open and we walked through
no biggie. The music was dumb as shit.
My girlfriend was wicked smart.

Skunked

Playing cribbage, drinking Heinekens
when a car pulls into father's yard.
Someone's here, I say. *Who is it?*
he asks. I don't know—you

find out, it's your house. *Oh
you know who that is? It's the fucking
Mormons or some Christly group,*
he says getting up, walking outside.

He returns. What did they want? I ask.
*I don't know. They had their Bibles
in their laps. Said we need to end
suffering in the world. They told me

I was suffering.* What did you say?
He settles into his chair and nods
at the window. *You can see them
pulling out the driveway, can't you?*

Skin

You know the scenery: fence
around the flower garden.

Bolt Stunner

Bob says the
slaughterhouse
animals piled
high as the ceiling.
In the cold
processing
plant sometimes
you saw trails
of warm air
rise from
somewhere
in the pile.
It was bad
work. One night
he stood face
to face with
a terrified
horse missing
a hoof, snorting,
cinched upright
so he shot it.

Dream Box

Father led her into the stall.
She shivered off flies.

*

Holding a knife to my throat,
Mother serving green beans with milk.

*

In love with a Bahá'í girl,
summer breeze and jasmine,
beginning to learn basic computing.

*

I kicked out the last window,
thumbed postcards of the Beatles in Miami.
The asbestos swirled in a hot cloud.

*

At the capitol,
everyone we knew dumped their yield
on the statehouse lawn.
Flies at the governor's window.

*

Far up the old town road
to the muddy lip of Job's Pond.
Peeled a leech from my ankle.

*

That winter Father fell out of the silo.
A black wire stretched across the road.

*

Everything was distant—Chicago, Mother's
tapping heel, music Father played
in a club on Church Street
before they made me by accident.

*

The therapist told me to lie on the floor
then walk the Welsh pony into the dump truck.
The next spring we sold the farm.

*

She pumped the bellows
and the coals leapt alive.
We tossed the football beside the forge.

Dennis Gonyaw

Grandfather's truck smelled
of Canadian mints and gasoline.
Dennis drove milk truck for years
after his wife died. Couldn't
stand walking to the barn alone

every morning, firing the whole
operation to life when the tractor
that crushed her sat on the slab,
ready to shove the day's shit
into the pit. And it piles up,

don't it. You have to remove it
because you can't live like that—
surrounded by shit. It's not
right. So he sold the business
and got a job visiting all his

neighbors. Dennis was the best
goddamn driver I ever rode with.
His truck had seventeen gears
and he could climb them all
and you'd never feel a thing.

Cheap Guitar

I will fix up
her guitar now
she is dead,
now it is no
longer a symbol

for how I felt
every day since.
Now it is just
an unused
instrument.

We received her
ashes in an urn
and brought them
home to our
windowsill.

I will bring her
guitar back
with a wet cloth
and new strings
for our concert

when we move
her urn to the
center of the
living room
and sing to her.

At the Cemetery

The most important thing—
conduct yourself with
courtesy. Don't talk.
Walk your dog quietly
on the November grass
in its mourning coat
of late-day light.
When the car appears
in private cortege
leave. Leave well enough
alone. Concede the yard.
Help grief to its privacy.
There is little to see—
a few tears, names
and dates so small
you bow to read them.

The Song Inside

You remember? Luke sees Leia
in the real first movie while
he's hanging out in the garage
setting up his horn—she pops out
the robot and he's like *Dang,
she's hot* and she's all *Save us,
Obi Wan*. Before he seriously
shed chops—before dedication,
boring as a desert. Soon
he's wondering whence
this song inside? and what exactly
is the real story about his pops—
bop killer who smoked everyone
on the bandstand. Just legend?
Legend doesn't satisfy the drive
to master mystery. Meeting
a father is epic. A father
gives his son what he knows
and may even reveal secrets
only guilt caused by love
can occasion. He'd remove
the mask, uncover Anakin—
purveyor of smooth jazz.
Mythology is bloodied by adults
who can't play together,
but father and son would maneuver
through any lingering dissonance
over a couple gigs, trading fours,

shoving and pulling against
each other's time—Luke all
No man, this is how we do it now
and Vader like *Join me.* Someday
the young Jedi might pull the horn
from his mouth and listen.

First on the Scene

I unbuckled and got out,
dodging traffic, remembering
the ride home from sister's
winter concert, creeping

the frozen miles back
to the farm in Father's
truck years before I knew
what work was. We rolled

up on the delivery van
nose down in the snowy
Clyde river, headlights
glowing in the black,

quiet water and the man
dead in coveralls belted
in his seat, arms hanging
like he was asking for a hug.

Highly Regarded

How does she do it? My wife is incredible.
However. Putting her things away when she's
done with them is not a strength. But she is
an awesome mom. No matter what—even when the
children rain vitriol on her. When they throw her
kindnesses in her face. When they humiliate
her. It is part of the job. She accepts it. She is
an expert advocate for them when they argue
with me, like a fucking lawyer. She pushes them
away from junk food but allows hot chocolate,
one part of her complex charm. She pushes them
to not give up on hard things. Like chapter books.
Like showing up to whatever it is. You are not
to be satisfied with being just ok because
you're better than that. When the children
stand at the podium of childhood achievement
scanning the crowd for her approval, they know
they can always find a flaw, strengthen a
weakness. Why. Because they are flawed.
But in a good way. She makes no apologies
for riding roughshod over their laziness
and into their business. She is expert with
apologetic kindness. Like a knife nicks your
Achilles. Her willingness to wheedle has,
we acknowledge, opened many doors for
this family do not forget it. She befriends
professors of literature and dances to their
condescension. Receives regards from

senators and CEOs. They do not distract
nor do they obscure her collection of empty
wine glasses, or the boxes on the stairwell,
the mountains of clothing, school work,
receipts, towelettes, packets of sugar, past-
due medical bills. She shows me the famous
photo of Einstein's office. It's a wreck. Mess
is a sign of creativity, she says. I would say that,
too, if my side of the room looked like hers.

Taking Our Son to College in the Morning

The storm gathered
hundreds of miles away
in a strange part of the world
but the weather map

projected a path over
our house. We knew someday
we'd sing the final melody
from our little nest,

knew our last goodnight
and good morning
would arrive.
We were too old to be

surprised but there we sat
side-by-side on the couch
in disbelief listening to the rain
and a birdcall from the dark.

Jeopardy

What if, when we are old and have lost interest
in our children and things scholarly, we become
what we strove so hard to avoid—comforted
by routine, scheduled by television. What is

the morning coffee you brewed while I slept?
Who is the woman who suffered my abuse?
What are conditions of indebtedness? And when
we cease using our names, or your health

causes an address to God who never crossed
the threshold of our house, what is *I will not
die first*? Who is the one most likely to bear
remaining days? We'll know the beauty

of a breath. One need only feel the air to know
what lies within the corpse-colored clouds.
Then forgetting begins: where you left your glasses
(on your head), forgetting when we first met

(the night I lit myself on fire), forgetting your
flawed iris, hair across a tile. Rain rolls through
the deltas of sand on the bank of Memphremagog
before joining the lake. What is an evening

of opposites? Who owns this lilac scented
letter? What are brief songs? Until then,
we live with small amounts, with want, a list
of questions for which we deserve no answer.

Cymbal

The old motorcycle
bought with money
from the sale of my
finest cymbal rests
in the barn with its
dead battery and a
nest of nude mice
beneath the chrome
fender with evening
growing darker and
cooler by the second.

Symbols

Before discussing "The Chrysanthemums" I draw
a cross on the blackboard. That's Jesus, says
Rob. A swastika: evil. A dollar sign: opportunity.
The American flag reminds Peg of patriotism.
The other Rob announces, oppression. Patrick
thinks it's marketing for the Fender Stratocaster.
You've got to have some presence, Gail says
(who told me before class it was her boyfriend
and his brother and his brother and his brother
and they could just give her their shit and what
the fuck was she going to do? Live on the street?
Nothing. And their mother, after Gail does the
laundry and cooks, says she's going to crack,
fail school. Tells her she's ugly. Gail says she
wants to punch someone. *I'm thirty-three and
don't own a car*). Colby says, Gail, can you please
save your sob story for Thursday? I keep the
window open—it is so hot in the classroom.
We fan our faces around the conference table.
I draw the lidded Salinas Valley. Gail fills her
notebook with unicorns on hind legs. Animals
often indicate symbolism, I say. Tracey notes
the dog under the junk wagon, lean, slow to
fight and that Elisa Allen is lean like the dog—
when her mums are kicked to the road she loses
hope. She loses hope, I repeat, asking Gail,
why can't she make herself happy? Gail laughs.
She doesn't even know how unhappy she is.

Animal Hospital

I don't recognize the decal
on the Mazda's rear window—
a star in a white bar. Something
military, for courage in battle,
loss of a child? I see the registration
is due, the driver knows
something about war, Veterans
Affairs is motivated by profit,
Snowden revealed secrets,
Congress is assembled by animus,
and through brindled shade
traffic moves easily north
up route 7a. At the animal hospital,
we see a bobcat's jaw. Chalky
bladder stones tumble noisily
from a jar onto an exam table.
We see x-rays of a broken tail,
a crushed paw, and four
long quills. We see a photo
of the dog with the quills
through its lip. It is trendy
to post photos of your wounds.
People like to see meaty,
bleeding lacerations
of other people. The dog
is on the hospital's homepage.
Below the operating theater,
a dozen more yip and stare

behind a maze of fences
at Doktor Doggy Daycare.
Staff patrols the curious
preschoolers, squirt bottles ready.
The final exhibit is a closet
that, by a magic of open doors,
becomes a cell. The children
shove inside and I snap a bird's
eye view. Charlie sticks out
his tongue. Josie makes a scary face.

University

Instagram feeds advice.
We are in full mourning.
Change rolls like waves
too far out to see.

How gentle, how tolerant
he's become. I rest my hand
on his shoulder. We burn
a fire at night,

watch sparks dart. *It's ok*
to make mistakes, I say
meaning who will
love me? *Pay attention*

to floods and smoke from
fires on distant mountains.
The world... His arms
around me. *Dad, I get it.*

Fair Game

I took first prize in the goat-milking contest
and was lifted to the back of an elephant
like some tiny god of the harvest. A father
knelt by his son and, pointing at me,
whispered in the lad's ear. The child
wet his pants, dropped his cotton candy,
and began to weep. As we swayed
regally through the crowd, I wiped
the milk from my fingers and slowly
raised my hands above my head.
In this posture was I carried from the arena.
It was a great day. We were nearing the midway
when a lady slid aside us, snagged my leg,
and brushed my knee with her beard.
My life is a tilt-a-whirl of nausea and dreams!
I cried. We could have been happy together
but I didn't know that then. I only knew
that time was shining, and tearing off
my overalls I burst into a cloud of pollen
and slowly floated over the dark barns.

Part 3

The Heart's Bones

The birds, I've heard them
a thousand times before
but they are still exotic
to me. It's not fair, all the ways
you can hate someone
by loving them. A twist,
as they say. One that
breaks the heart's bones.
My daughter wonders
how soft a pet bunny
would be. So soft, so
soft—she savors the
words. I saved a squirrel
from the neighbor's
netting. These three
blueberry bushes—
a few weeks each year
they are chests of sapphires.
The birds will ruin them,
they told me. Their son
was born premature.
They sound cheerful in the
group chat but I know—
my first son almost died.
Yesterday he saved two
cardinals from that
damn net. And today the
grey squirrel catching

its useless claws.
I yanked the net up,
expecting it to roll
like a barrel onto the grass.
But it held on like
I wanted to kill it.

Meagre Objects

This poem begins in Alaska where
they name their kids Maverick and
Hunter and Trig which is short for
Trigger but I always hear as Twig
like what you find all over the floor
in Alaska next to a pair of boots
in the ready position near the door
because conditions are always
extreme in Alaska where the animals
are white and the enormous chips of ice
floating in the sea are slushy and blue.
One of many subjects about which
I know very little. My Alaskan neighbors
say everyone there rolls their own
cigarettes and their eyes at that fool
Chris McCandless who ruined
himself eating some natty berries.
I wonder if every Alaskan could go
into the darkness of their failure and
live off the meagre objects they find.
My neighbors followed the pipeline
back to the USA unlike McCandless
and eventually to Vermont where
everything is green and the color
of dying leaves. Everything (I bought
for Secret Santa) comes from the soil—
wine, chocolate, and succulents from
the hardware store. I was sure to not

overspend (sorry Anne). The plant
was sprayed red. Funds are always
strained in human services and I still
came in way under budget. Thrift
is a value Alaskans cultivate in their
young. They eat the whole fish.
Across three states and fifty-two
years I caught three. This poem
addresses things of which I know
little. What I know about fish
I learned from Elizabeth Bishop
who caught one risking its long and
hard-fought life so she could train
her shy, drunken gaze over its body.
Once she let that mysterious object
slip from her hands and back into
the blue sea with those imaginary
rainbows the poem was done.

To Things Left Behind

The note on the butcher block
says Tuesday, 1:10 pm.

Forks and spoons in the drying rack
beg me to return them
to their coffins.

Your shoes frown across the den.

In the bathroom,
the light spots my mouth's muster

of white lies, the mirror, the crack
of your hair on the tile floor tells me
you will be back,

tells me you never left
the long relief of your clothes

at the foot of the bed. All night,
light reveals the front door,

the mask the chorus speaks behind.
I leave it on.

In Situ

Maybe the answer was music,
wind through a stand of trees,
rain on the barn roof. He wanted
to know, back there, in his seat,

Daddy, what is more important—
music or trees? I thought about
night that seemed to lie suddenly
on the long, cold grass and when

it was too dark how sounds of
the world announced the world,
the words of things—wings of
a crow, the snap of limbs.

Even his own breath made
a sound but Jesus he was only
four and a half. He didn't know
about hard-borne sap rising

and falling through vascular
cambium in the sugar bush
on the hill or how skin breathes
and roots pull water from

the earth. I thought about loss
of leaves, of light, how tides
of air press in the invisible sky,
the dark sky, moments

of shade when the mind finds
correlation with an object,
in this case a tree nearly
thrown down, wind hissing

in pine limbs years ago when
I was a little older than him
and walked back and back
to the topmost field, the night

pasture, and sat stone-still while
the world wove afternoon into
late afternoon and the sun
sank into the cedar swamp.

History of Square Dancing

Early 1942, Hiram moved to California
to pick fruit, gone two years. Hazel taught

her students: Gettysburg, the Somme,
dictators and dates. *Pass through.*

Hiram came home, left two months later
for the shipyards in Bath, hot-riveting

destroyers. *Pass the ocean, pass the sea.*
He returned each autumn to cut the rowen.

Forward and back. Every weekend,
Hazel and Hiram went dancing at Paul's

Sugar House. *Cast a shadow.* Hazel stands,
lays down her whist hand, heads out

for a cigarette. They tried farming
on Five Mile Square Road till Hiram,

now husband, shot himself in their trailer
kitchen. *Bow to your partner.*

Hazel drops her butt and twists it
with her toe. Inside, the caller calls

promenade left and the dancers circle.
Partner trade and courtesy turn. Hay bales,

plaid shirts, spinning floral skirts. Liberty,
first name John, swings her under.

Winter Fuel

The last thing I did
when grandfather
was on his bed, dying
in his clothes—hold
his left uncovered foot
in the early morning dark.
Cats leaping on the bed
wake me from the dream.
They hunt the mouse
beneath my chest. Then
morning is a pale glow,
the first snow has fallen
on the yard, on the cars,
on the young birch,
bending it like a rude
child should be bent,
they thought when this
house was built—you
taught respect. Many
couples laid in this oddly
illumined room before
we bought a mortgage.
What a lovely dead-end,
we thought. Mature
landscaping. The kids
will be safe. Last night
another limb broke off
the old cherry tree—

be prepared, you said,
to wake some morning
and find the whole thing
sprawled over the snow.

The Summer My Sister Channeled the Spirit World

Behind a closed door, secrets, wisdom,
page after page—a new voice, a face
under deep water, long sentences
forecasting who she would love, why,
and why they did not yet love her.
Her hand slanted anew as though
she was half-turned, listening to
someone outside a window, behind
a door. That summer she received
an old, unbroken pony that threw her
in the yard, threw her in the field.
I threw bales in the meadow and loft
while she laid-out on the roof,
painting her nails, applying lotion
under the wild July sunshine
bouncing off the shingles. We circled
the table and she appeared, silent
in shades. Sixteen, listening to
Foreigner. She sipped sweet tea,
angry at the fields and fences,
the mountains all around, the scent
of manure in her clothes and hair.
She snapped open her Walkman,
flipping the tape in rhythm and sighed
a sigh about needing friends nearby,
boys, parties in town. I watered
calves at night, the barn ringing

with the sound of cold chains.
Then she was gone to college,
purchased a futon and spider plants
for her purple room in the basement
apartment, bouncing major to major,
field to field—how to tape an ankle
sprain, sketch a nude from life,
and beneath garish lights cut open
a cadaver to see everything that
makes the body live and nothing
that makes it human.

Span

She was there, silent as a rag doll.
I unpinned her calendar from the wall.
A busy year until early May—
a hair appointment the very day
someone took her out in a bag.
Years were crumbs, absence sound.
She didn't say a word. I heard her
everywhere. You watched
from the window but she
didn't appear. When we arrived
and opened the door
for a second I believed
she'd just run to the store.
She wasn't coming back.
Or hadn't completely gone,
I couldn't tell. With my finger
I upset the little bells on the porch,
expecting to hear her call my name.
Instead, the kids wanted to know—
Dad, can we watch a show?
and scattered to the blue corners
of her couch. I occupied
an empty chair, surveyed the room:
wool blankets she threw
over the bannister, the quiet
Baldwin upright in the corner.
Her collection of keys
in a basket on the piano bench.
She never told me what they meant.

Father's Desk

In heavy side drawers unlocked, keys
lost, in files, hanging deep, a history
in numbers, soil sample test results,

grain freshen dates, dates served,
sire names—Winston, Teddy, Master
Goodman, herd locations, medical

costs, culling counts, vet numbers,
rent a bull, feedstore, blacksmith,
fuel delivery, saw dust. Vigorous

facts exhausted, entered late in life,
late to chores, past moonrise and past
dark barns, in a summer of death,

an unsatisfied winter, heifers caught
in the barbed wire, blood on snow,
cow down in the quarter piece,

prolapsed uterus, stillborn calf on
a square bale, slash, question mark,
asterisk. The center drawer

(pulled out), erasers, pens, sharp
pencils, paper clips, records daily
updated, columns of figures, pounds

of milk produced per cow, herd
averages, price per hundred weight.
Decisive seven months of increasing

yields, declining revenue. Teaching
career long since surrendered to
carry forward the family endeavor,

modernize systems, computerize
feed schedules, rotate crops, improve
drainage. The state took it all except

these documents, dot matrix
evidence of one more small farm
whited out, filed away, folded.

La Vie en Rose

We scraped the Mississippi mud
off our old piano and Father

blew his solos out the open window
and over the meadow

and Mother made me strut
with her double-stops, drum sticks

in hand, the old rhythms
of everything I hadn't learned

but was sure I heard bouncing
off the mountains in my head.

Fleas marched across
the saint-filled rug. It wasn't

sorrowful to travel somewhere
new, that's what the music said.

I was moved—some nights
unsure where here was.

Beale Street? Indiana? I lived
five miles outside town,

cow piss in my boot.
My splash cymbal ached to punch

the end of every tune.
We shook hands and I shivered

with joy—it was real,
living, our family band.

Against Feeling

I hear the world
with eyes rolled

back. You crunch
in the snow outside.

The doorknob
twists, and the teeth

that lock it
grind together.

The Lesson

Grandfather didn't know my back—
the place where the trunk twisted

when he delivered my nine spanks—
was like an old man's. Nerves and muscles

sent me back to the wrestling mat—
some ill-paired meet with a bigger kid

from another school whose chin
was razor-burn red. No calling it off,

though I was terrified. He gathered me
in his arms and threw me to the mat.

I twisted to escape but was pinned,
back sprained. I screamed

at grandfather *Get off!* and slapped
his arms away. He stood,

said something wounded as adults will
when a child reveals their mistake,

and walked to the barn,
not speaking to me for five days.

Me, who wanted to know everything
the old man appeared to know;

who always wanted to hear about
his handstand on the barn roof;

or the time he fell under the truck
and lived to tell; or his fight

with the four sailors who whistled
at his first wife. For five days

we did chores in silence, side by side:
one washing, the other drying

milk machines. I watched him
pull the levers of the silo motor,

listened to the elevator grind,
watched the serpentine belt dump silage,

cows darting for the trough, slamming
their skulls. Then I hobbled through

the shit and piss that was everywhere
to beg his forgiveness.

Asleep

*You're in for a rude
awakening,* she
predicted. The world
was going to slap

the grin off me
and she was going
to be there to see it.
The rudest

awakening came
the night she died
in her sleep and
I was shaken

from my dream
of work and money
while she missed
the whole thing.

Scrimshaw

Though one is an ocean the other
is not the fish. One will be the sail

bursting with wind, the other
will be the flag appearing and

disappearing behind obscure waves.
One will be timber and rigging,

the other mystifying knots tied
to time. One of us will surely be

the iron cannon shaking the deck,
the ever dry fuse. One will become

flotsam, sailors in the riptide,
smoke billowing. One is captain,

the other a gangrenous foot.
One is the Man of War and

the other is the Lady of the Lake.
One is sunk. The other lists

beneath the crowd of tourists.
One will be the scratch of

drowning rats. One will be
the overwhelming sea entering

the vessel. One is the broken ship
settling into the dark and the other

is crushing pressure. And names
of ships are etched on bone where

ships lean, manned in throaty
screams of pretend motion.

And the monument is carved.
Balloons sail over the crowd.

The band beats a cadence. One
will be the veteran of something

nearly forgotten. The other will have
no memory of all the killing.

Picking Stone

I call this one the empty bag of money
and this one trip to Vegas, pocket aces,
lacy windows, honeymoon suite. Hot day
kiss my back. Here—I call this some
bizarre unknown changed life, a wife,
a perfect afternoon. Here—this sweltering
dirt field. I'm what fifteen or something
dreamy? You can see this bucketful,
load weight . . . Exacta to win, gin, juniper,
madness of rock, stock, barrel. Skin,
my skin. Little flesh like fresh paint
peeling under the weight of work, so
my little glass of water, so my little breeze.
I call this one Mother, this Father.
How have you been? Let's begin
by jumping ship. I call this clipper wind, port.
Avenue of doting white pine, this is family
and ancestor and custom and control
over a bowel function slipping away.
This is artifact, way, a being mere memory,
mere tradition. And still picking stone,
still heat. Wind whipping this field up
and over the trees; each stone's smoke signal—
what language to inject in this contract,
this epilogue? Goodbye yard and Guernsey
and Brown Swiss and Jersey.
What's the impression of a field wall?
Blood, blister open, oozing on a handle,

an eye lashed on the woods road. Blood
on a sheet, son, you will know nothing
of that New England, that field, those buildings,
routine, pounds of produce, milk, meat of earth.

About the Author

JEFF McRAE lives in Vermont with his wife and three children. He earned a Masters in Writing from the University of New Hampshire and a Masters in Fine Arts in poetry from Washington University, St. Louis where he was the recipient of the Academy of American Poets prize. Since returning to Vermont, he's worked as a fly rod builder, a digital marketing copywriter, a youth employment specialist, and for fifteen years as a creative writing and literature instructor. Along the way he's served as poetry reader for *Boulevard Magazine* and *The Adroit Journal*. His poetry has appeared in *Massachusetts Review*, *Antioch Review*, *Rattle*, *Salamander*, and many other publications. He has been a finalist for several first book awards including the New Issues Poetry Prize, the Gerald Cable Book Award, and the Cider Press Review Book Award. An active musician, he also performs in theaters, clubs, and concert halls throughout New England.

www.ingramcontent.com/pod-product-compliance
Lightning Source LLC
Chambersburg PA
CBHW030050100426
42734CB00038B/997